Dingle Peninsula • County Kerry

Little Books of Ireland

Book and Jacket Design by Brian Murphy

Photography © by Liam Blake

© Picture Press.ie Ltd 2013

Published by Real Ireland Design
Picture House
16/17 Bullford Business Park,
Kilcoole, County Wicklow.
www.realireland.ie
info@realireland.ie

A CIP catalogue record for this book is available from the British Library.

ISBN 0946887-705

No part of this publication may be reproduced, stored in a retrieval system or transmitted in any form or by any means, electronic, mechanical, photocopying, scanning or otherwise, without prior permission of the copyright owner.

Storm • West Cork

Donkeys and dry stone wall • Aran Islands

Mullaghmore • County Sligo

Ross Castle • Killarney • County Kerry

The Hook lighthouse • County Wexford

Dingle Peninsula • County Kerry

Giant's Causeway • County Antrim

Skellig Michael • County Kerry

Winter Glendalough • County Wicklow

Cliffs of Moher • County Clare

Poulnabrone Dolmen • The Burren • County Clare

Dun Aengus • Aran Islands

Ballinahinch • Connemara

Beara Peninsula • West Cork

Roundstone • Connemara

Achill • County Mayo

Derryclare Lough • Connemara

The Worm Hole • Aran Islands

Carrick-a-Rede • County Antrim

Waterville • County Kerry

Sea Stacks • County Donegal

Dunluce Castle • County Antrim

Skellig Lighthouse • County kerry

Sea Cliffs • Aran Islands

Gannets • Saltee Islands • County Wexford

Twelve Bens Mountains • Connemara

Big Wave Surfers • County Clare

Glenveigh • County Donegal

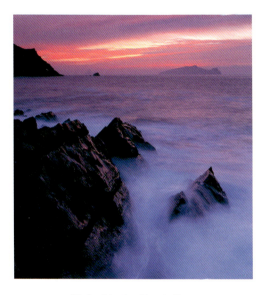

Blasket Islands • County Kerry

Atlantic Puffins